5-Minute Daily Meditations

5-MINUTE DAILY MEDITATIONS

Instant Wisdom, Clarity & Calm

SAH D'SIMONE

ALTHEA
PRESS

This book is an offering of love and forgiveness to everyone.
I trust this book will serve as a reminder that you're worth the effort,
that you're worthy of freedom. May all beings be happy.

CONTENTS

THE JOURNEY BACK TO YOUR HEART

T hank you for picking up this book and taking a step in the direction of well-being for your mind, body, and soul. It is an honor for me to help guide you as you embark on your journey toward greater peace, calm, and wisdom.

My name is Sah D'Simone. Today I'm a meditation teacher and transformational coach with an emphasis on contemplative psychotherapy, but in my former life, I was the creative director and co-founder of an international high-fashion magazine. The lifestyle that came with the magazine's success included celebrities, parties, and high-society living. On the outside, I had achieved the standard of success society told me should be my goal.

On the inside, however, something was crying out for attention, for help. Every morning I would feel a nagging ache in my chest. Instead of attending to it, I pushed it aside, trying to distract myself from it with more work, partying, drugs, and alcohol. But no matter how many ways I tried to avoid my inner pain, it always returned.

Then, suddenly and without warning, I was forced out of my company. In a single day, everything I had worked for, all of the markers of success I had accumulated, everything that I'd thought was real and permanent, vanished. All that remained was the inner turmoil that I'd been trying to ignore for so long. It was a terrifying place to be—dark, uncertain, and most of all, lonely.

I was empty and isolated. Everything felt meaningless. Depression sank its claws into me. Guilt, shame, and fear led me to contemplate suicide.

It took me five years and multiple trips to India and Nepal to learn how to address my depression. I studied with meditation teachers, healers, scientists, and spiritual masters—all of whom helped me understand my mind and how to cope with my human experience. But the most important journey I made during that time did not take me to the other side of the world: It took me back to my own heart, which I had been away from for far too long.

My journey was long and arduous, but yours doesn't have to be. You don't need to travel overseas or go on lengthy spiritual retreats to come in closer contact with your heart. You can do so wherever you are right now, by taking just a few minutes each day to pause, to notice, to feel, to reflect, to come into the present and rest for a moment.

This book is my invitation for you to do just that—to take one step back toward your heart every day for the next year. It offers 365 simple meditations incorporating breath work, mantra, reflection, affirmation, and visualization. Though this book is structured around the calendar year, it is also designed for you to be able to start your journey on any day. The right time to start is right now. You have the freedom to work through the meditations in this book in whatever way works best for you. Each practice can be done in just five minutes, at any time of day, and in just about any setting. It doesn't matter when or where you choose to do a practice; all that matters is that you choose to do it.

In touching base with your heart each day, you'll also learn how to make friends with your mind. The mind is the catalyst of both suffering and happiness. We are human beings, and pain and pleasure are inevitable parts of our experience. But it is what our mind tells us about our experiences that creates endless suffering.

The meditation practices in this book can help you see and better understand the inner workings of your mind. In the traditional sense, meditation is a simple concentration process that changes how we relate to ourselves and our surroundings. It leads us away from the agitated, chaotic internal dialogue of the mind and into a full experience of the present moment. We learn that whatever we're experiencing does not define our lives or who we are, but is just one of many passing moments. We learn that our moods change just like the seasons, and no matter what our internal weather, we can always return to our calm center. From there, we can approach everything that comes up with spaciousness, resilience, and playfulness, which leads to insight, forgiveness, and unconditional love.

I can't promise that you'll stop experiencing tough, painful emotions altogether. But I can promise that by taking just five minutes each day, it is possible for you to gently undo the little destructive mind patterns that make you suffer and to find your way back to your calm inner center and live from there.

Welcome to the journey back to your heart.

PART ONE
Beginning

JANUARY

STARTING OVER

1

JANUARY

Let Go of the Past

"Today I choose to uncouple from my past and align myself with the highest harmonies. May this open me up to experience my essence and invoke my power."

Keep this intention in mind throughout the day, and observe how the universe responds to you.

2
JANUARY

Taking Responsibility

We often do things that we don't want to do. Then when we become unhappy with the choices we've made, we blame life and others for where we find ourselves. What if, instead, you were to take personal responsibility for how the path of your life is unfolding, and no longer blame the world if you dislike it?

Consciously do your best to rebuild your mind-set in this way. If you get off course and start blaming other people and things, forgive yourself and start again—and again and again—as many times as you need.

3
JANUARY

Thoughts Are Predictable

Thoughts will think themselves without any help from you.
So you can just sit back and watch them do their thing.

4

JANUARY

Who Are You?

Imagine you are no longer any of your roles. You're no longer defined by your job role or your family role as a child, a sibling, a parent. You're no longer defined by the pain and hurt you've been through.

Who are you now? Allow the answers to come to you.

5

JANUARY

It's Right Here

Our inherent qualities of goodness and love are always with us—
as close to us as our breath.

6

Rebirth Affirmation

"Today I'm reborn in a totally different way.
I have the inner strength to cultivate
patience and wisdom."

7

Higher Intelligence

Enter the gap between thoughts, between breaths. It is in that space that
you have access to pure potential and that you come into closer contact
with your heart. It is there that an intelligence beyond your wildest
imagination arises.

8

Point of Refuge Meditation

Find a comfortable meditation position—a posture that balances wakefulness and relaxation, such as sitting upright in a comfortable chair with your hands calmly resting in your lap. Gently let your eyes close, and take a few long deep breaths to land back into your body.

Now visualize a line connecting the point between your eyebrows to the bottom of your spine. Use this connecting line as the object of focus for this meditation. If at any time you catch your mind wandering, gently and kindly invite it back to the line. Rest here for five minutes.

Use this line as your point of refuge throughout your day. When you feel disconnected from yourself, imagine this line again within you.

9
JANUARY

No Splitting

You can't live in the past and the present at the same time. Honor how the past has affected you, yet stay open to the present moment and all its possibilities. Throughout the day, notice if you're splitting your attention and trying to engage with the past and the present at the same time.

10
JANUARY

Integration Instead of Separation

Your natural impulse is to love deeply, to help, to connect. However, the stories you tell yourself when those impulses arise keep you trapped in the old habits of separation. With the support of your breath, you can realign with your heart and become aware of the moments you choose to separate instead of integrate. Awareness will allow you to make a different choice.

Fresh Start Mantra Meditation

Take a deep breath in through your nose, resting your attention on your breath for a few moments. And then engage the breath and the mind together.

Breathing in, say: *Today I commit to approaching everything with a beginner's mind.*

Breathing out, say: *I choose to enter the day with wonder.*

Breathing in: *I choose to open myself to new possibilities.*

Breathing out: *I choose to remain curious.*

Breathing in: *I choose to notice details I don't normally see.*

Breathing out: *I choose to not compare what I am experiencing to a previous experience.*

12
JANUARY

Be Someone's Luck

Become someone's luck today by bestowing on them
a random act of kindness.

13
JANUARY

Seeing Clearly Affirmation

"The more in touch I am
with myself, the closer
I am to reality as it is."

14
JANUARY

Loving-Kindness Meditation: Patience

This meditation is an adaptation of a classic Buddhist meditation called the *metta* (or loving-kindness) meditation.

Start by resting your attention on the feeling of the breath in the body. Then gently repeat these phrases to yourself:

May I be patient.

May I be patient with my family.

May I be patient with everyone I come in contact with.

Now notice how you feel. Repeat this practice throughout your day, whenever you begin to feel impatient.

15
JANUARY

—

The Not-So-Secret Map

Within all of us is the blueprint to the life of our dreams. Our work is to uncover this hidden map and live by following it. What makes you feel alive? Do that. It will lead the way to your next step—and the next and the next.

16
JANUARY

—

Affirmation for Change

"Today I stop coming back to what doesn't feel good. I stop allowing my mind to be untrained. I stop allowing negative thinking to take over. Today I can change. Today I am change."

17
JANUARY

Open Focus Meditation

Begin by checking in with your posture, making sure it is comfortable and at ease. Allow the eyes to close or lightly gaze at a space ahead of you.

With a few deep breaths, welcome yourself into this moment.

Open up your field of awareness, observing with a fresh set of "eyes," everything that is passing through your mind. Allow each thought to simply come and go. Becoming an objective observer of your mind allows you to find the space between you and your thoughts.

18
JANUARY

It Is a Choice

You can either fall into the trap of fear or break the cycle of fear.

19

JANUARY

We All Benefit

Your personal healing is helping everyone around you heal.

20

JANUARY

Body Scan Meditation: Abdominal Area

Start by bringing your attention to the sensations of breath in your body.

Now direct your attention to your abdominal area. Perhaps you notice sensations of hunger. What stories come up with that? Perhaps you notice sensations of digestion. What stories come up with that?

Notice what there is to be felt in your abdominal area. If there is nothing, notice that as well.

Simply become aware of the sensations in this one part of the body. Bring awareness to your abdominal area, one breath at a time.

21
JANUARY

Personal Responsibility Affirmation

"Today I stop being a passive part of my inner experience. I choose to not get carried away in self-hate, unconscious forms of hate toward others, and guilt for not living up to society's standards of 'enough.'
I am aware that the more I believe these thoughts playing in my mind, the further from the truth I am. It's time to say goodbye to all the inner noise. I am enough, and I am trying my best. I listen to the inner voices that support this knowing."

22
JANUARY

One Act of Power

What would happen if you raised your expectations for yourself? Today, can you commit to dropping one limiting belief that disempowers you, and do one thing that makes you feel energized and powerful? You are your only limit!

23
JANUARY

Natural Discernment

You know the difference between truth and fabrication.

24
JANUARY

Subtle but Powerful

Today, observe your impulses. Become aware of old patterns rooted in agitation, confusion, and impatience. Perhaps you have the tendency to snap at loved ones or become irritated with a certain coworker. Or maybe you become filled with rage when you hit traffic every day after work.

Remember that you have a choice when an impulse like this arises. With the support of your breath, you have the power to slow down and tune into the gaps between the stimulus and response—where solutions live.

25
JANUARY

Make Peace with the Past

Be at peace with all that you have done thus far in this lifetime.

26
JANUARY

The Road Home

The journey from the mind into the heart is your daily practice. Let go of unhappy thoughts and negative emotions, and come back into the home base, to the heart.

27
JANUARY

What You're Not

When you're caught up in negative thoughts or emotions about yourself or other people, you're disconnected from your truth. You are not your thoughts; you're the listener. You are not your emotions; you're the observer. Every time you notice that you're entangled in a stream of negativity, it's a sign that you need to realign with your true self and come back to the present by feeling your breath in your body.

28
JANUARY

Your Stories Create Your Life

Take this opportunity to observe the stories you've been carrying around and keep telling yourself. Start a new chapter.

29
JANUARY

Me, Myself, and I

Spending time alone—without distractions or ways to avoid feeling alone— invites a direct experience with the core of your being. True aloneness is an opportunity to take inventory of what might be cluttering your connection to yourself and others. Real aloneness is sacred time, when you can integrate your heart with your mind and body.

30
JANUARY

Tasting the Truth

Stop pretending the past is real by attaching yourself to what happened in it. The constant craving for the "good old days" or the tendency to cling to negative memories pulls you away from the truth. The truth is what you are experiencing in this present moment.

Take a few minutes to be in the present moment. A simple way to do this is to say to yourself, "Now I am . . ." For example, if I am doing laundry, I tell myself, "Now I am doing laundry."

31
JANUARY

Underneath Thoughts

Appreciate periods free of mental chatter, however rare they are. When you become one with the present moment, you have access to beauty, abundance, creativity, and infinite potential beyond what you could ever imagine.

FEBRUARY

SELF-LOVE

1
FEBRUARY

Loving-Kindness Meditation: Love

Start by resting your attention in the feeling of the breath in the body. Then gently repeat these phrases:

May I be love.

May I offer love.

May I receive love.

Now notice how you feel. Repeat this meditation throughout your day, to remind yourself of your loving intention.

2
FEBRUARY

Nonattachment

It is possible to see things without attaching feelings to them.

3

Your Dreams Matter

As adults, we can forget to dream. Grant yourself permission to dream again. What do you dream for yourself? And do you believe that your dream matters? Your dreams matter because they are the key to unlocking your human potential, which is what you are here to do. Even if your dreams feel completely outrageous, just remember how miraculous it is that you're here right now, reading these words in a human body. What a dream you already are! What a miracle your life already is!

4

FEBRUARY

Out of the Cage

Don't be a prisoner of your assumptions when you meet other people. Instead, meet them with a beginner's mind, free of unconscious biases.

―――

Your Inherent Magic

Who are the people, where are the places, and what are the things in your life that awaken magic in you?

You might find it helpful to write down these three categories.

Gently connect with your breath for a few moments, feeling it in your body, then write down the answers as they come to you. Now ask yourself, how can I spend more time in the places and with the people and things that awaken me?

―――

Mirrors

When you see your own goodness, you can see the goodness in others. Never forget that we are all born good.

7

Be a Magnet

People are naturally drawn to those who have a heart filled with compassion and peace. These shining ones carry wisdom and grace. Follow them.

And be one yourself. Be someone who spreads peace. Show peace in everything you do. Breathe peace. Be peace. Live peace.

8

FEBRUARY

You Work Better as We

Ask for help. Reach out. Don't be afraid of how you're perceived. You're serving as an example for others, giving them permission to do the same.

9

FEBRUARY

Just One Healing Thing

Taking the first step toward your healing can feel hard, and you are the only one who can do it. Take agency of your life by doing one thing each day to support your healing. You can do one thing. You know you can.

Here are some ideas: Take a bath. Breathe deeply for a few minutes. Call a good friend. Listen to music you love. Visit a bookstore and let yourself be drawn to a new book. Buy yourself flowers. Take a yoga class. Take a nap. Take a walk around the block. Journal for five minutes.

What one healing thing can you do for yourself today?

10
FEBRUARY

Laughing Your Way to Enlightenment

When you experience a moment of grace, where your internal landscape falls silent and the inner critic is gone, rejoice in that freedom. Laugh at yourself for believing the stories that played out in your mind. Laugh with yourself for being wiser than you were yesterday. Laughing reconnects you to your body and the present moment.

11
FEBRUARY

Sexual Healing

Gather all of your attention and rest it on your sexual organ(s), taking a few deep breaths and channeling them to those pleasure points. Now repeat in your mind, "I release all shame, guilt, and fear. And I welcome love and kindness."

12
FEBRUARY

Are You Really Listening?

You're here to listen with your heart—not your ears or your mind. As you're listening to someone speak, notice whether you're crafting your response before they're even finished speaking. If you are, you're not really listening to them.

At these times, practice coming back to the feeling of your breath and then offer yourself fully—again and again—to the person you're listening to.

13
FEBRUARY

The Eyes of Enlightenment

How you think others see you is a story you tell yourself. How you think you see yourself is actually your attachment to past stories, and those stories are not true. How your heart sees yourself is absolute truth.

14
FEBRUARY

Don't Resist

Each time you choose to hold back from expressing your inherent qualities, you are stopping the flow of the universal current of miracles and wonder. Catch yourself when you are resisting the impulse to call someone just to say, "I love you." Then call that person. Catch yourself when you're resisting the impulse to smile at someone on the street. Then smile at that person. Catch yourself when you're resisting the impulse to get to know a stranger. Then get to know that person.

15
FEBRUARY

You Have a Legacy

How do you want to be remembered? What will live on when you no longer have your job, money, clothes, and all the stuff that you relied on to make up the stories you hoped other people saw you living? What outshines all that is the depth of your love. How will you love today?

16
FEBRUARY

———

Honoring Partnerships

May all your partnerships, friends, and lovers be inspirations for clear and honest communication. May they be signs to not take others for granted, but to treat them and yourself with respect. May they remind you often of what brought you together.

17
FEBRUARY

———

Listen to the Song of the Heart

Today, investigate matters of the heart.

With the support of your breath and an intention backed with love, ask yourself, "What is my heart's desire?" And allow the answer to come to you.

18

Breath Awareness Sitting Meditation

Take a comfortable seat, your spine long and upright yet relaxed. Allow your gaze to rest softly on a spot just ahead of you, or close your eyes. Rest your hands where they feel most comfortable.

Start to shift your attention from the thinking process to the inner strength of your breath. Practice tracing the breath in and out of the body for five minutes. If at any moment you notice your attention has been pulled away into the thinking process, kindly invite it back to trace the path of the breath.

When you're done, take a moment to notice what it's like inside you right now. For example, are you aware of your heart beating? Of an itch somewhere on your body? Do you feel warm? Are you aware of your breath? Notice everything in your physical experience.

19
FEBRUARY

Self-Acceptance Affirmation

"I love and accept myself just as I am."

20
FEBRUARY

Dear Difficult People. . .

Today, say to all the challenging people in your life, "Thank you for helping me exercise my best qualities: Compassion, kindness, courage, and calmness. I love you and honor you! I'm doing my best to see myself in all of you."

21
FEBRUARY

Friends Affirmation

Today I wish for friends who remind me of my inherent goodness, despite how we have been hardwired to believe that we are not good or that we are broken and not worthy.

Today I wish for friends who love me deeply and profoundly and, by offering me their presence and grace, make time for me to unravel my story and find my true feelings.

Today I wish for friends who are wise, smart, and fierce—friends who inspire me to do better each day.

Today I wish for friends who encourage me to explore untouched territory within myself.

Today I wish for friends who accept my imperfection without a single drop of judgment.

Today I wish for friends who remind me of my inherent compassion.

22
FEBRUARY

From Me to We

A selfless act done for the benefit of others is a profound, heart-opening practice. Compassionate, altruistic acts remind us that we are interconnected with all beings. Do something for someone else today. Notice your heart opening: This is what connection feels like.

23
FEBRUARY

People Who Help Us Heal

When you meet someone who continuously helps you exercise your best qualities—someone who helps you move through the valley of shadows toward the light, someone who can meet you at the space of deep inner silence, someone who shares the same aspirations to better themselves and the world—keep them close and reflect all of those things back to them.

24
FEBRUARY

Body Scan Meditation: Heart Center

Come into a comfortable seated position or, if you prefer, lie on your back.

Start by taking a few deep breaths.

Breathe in a sense of peace. On the out breath, let go of any tension.

Gather your attention into your chest and heart center area. Explore this area: What emotions are there to be noticed?

Experience a sense of compassion within your heart center. Notice sensations of warmth, of openness.

With a caring and open mind, one breath at the time, allow all emotions to be what they are. Gently notice them, and let them go.

25
FEBRUARY

Weird Is Good

Life is a profound miracle, and it must be lived like it is. Surround yourself with people who bring out the magic in you—the weird ones who show you new experiences and help break your old habits, who make you laugh out loud in public, who speak from the heart always. Make every day count, and add something to life every day! And most important of all, once you've figured out how to operate from that place, share the secret with everyone. Because the secret to living well is giving.

26
FEBRUARY

The Current Situation

Your relationship with the present moment is what defines who you are. It shows you the truth about your situation.

27

Courage Invocation

Today, ask yourself how you can help stop hate. Perhaps hate is manifesting as a feeling you have toward some part of yourself, or maybe it is reflected in the world at large or closer to home in your community. Is there one thing you can do differently today to inspire compassion and courage—in yourself or in others?

Today you are part of the change.

Today you have the courage to take the initiative,

The courage to say no,

The courage to take responsibility,

The courage to learn from your mistakes,

The courage to apologize,

The courage to let go of the past,

Continued

The courage to help others,

The courage to keep your commitments,

The courage to ask for help,

The courage to love yourself,

The courage to live with integrity,

The courage to challenge your stories,

The courage to dream bigger,

The courage to be who you are,

The courage to speak up,

The courage to open your heart fully,

The courage to be a leader.

28
FEBRUARY

The Real You

We constantly present ourselves to the world as convincing actors. We're so good that we often believe the lies we so benignly tell about how we really feel every day. How many times have you been asked, "How are you?" and responded with, "Good," when you were far from good?

While we have to do what we have to do to function socially and professionally, it's important to stay aware of the true feelings beneath the faces we present to the world.

Take a few minutes to answer the question for yourself: How are you *really*? Check in with yourself often. When we practice being present, real, and authentic, we drop the habitual acting, and we get to face ourselves with clarity. We give ourselves the privilege of knowing ourselves deeply while also being who we need to be in the world.

MARCH

ALIGNMENT

1

MARCH

Don't Believe Everything You Think

Liberation begins the moment you reestablish the witness to the thinking process and claim your power in the position of observer. Do not believe everything you think, and know that the more you believe your thoughts, the further away from the truth you are.

2

MARCH

Inner Booster

Each of us has a chorus of inner voices speaking to us at any given moment. Which inner voice should you listen to? The one that sounds like a cheerleader.

3
MARCH

Parenting Yourself

Have you ever noticed feelings of anger and envy arising within you when you see someone with a caring mother or father? So many of us didn't grow up with a nurturing parental presence, so that idea might not be something you're familiar with, and you may even have an aversion to it because of parental neglect.

You are worthy of living free of painful memories. Are you willing to forgive and stop operating from a place of shame and unworthiness?

With the support of your breath, collect your attention and combine it with a loving intention to open up your heart and parent yourself with patience, tenderness, and empathy.

4
MARCH

Authenticity Is How You Find Your People

Do us all a favor: Please don't hide your magic.
It's the only way for others to find you.

5
MARCH

Your Dreams Are Coming True

Are you familiar with your self-sabotaging mechanisms? Have you noticed that as you get closer to manifesting your dreams into reality, you start to feel unworthy or not ready? If you give space to those thoughts and feelings, and if you believe them, they become real.

Practice observing your thoughts, feelings, and dreams. When your intention becomes polluted and you start to lose contact with your mission, come back to your breath and repeat to yourself, "I am worthy of living my dreams."

6
MARCH

The Gift of the Unknown

Allow the mystery, admire the mystery, live the mystery. How boring would life be if you knew what the future held? It's a gift that each moment is full of potential and surprise.

7
MARCH

Permission to Come as You Are

Today, show up hiding nothing. Show up vulnerable and broken, with all of your suffering and pain, shame and guilt, loss and fear, anger and denial, lust and cruelty, mistakes and indifferences. Today, acknowledge all the old wounds and do your best to create enough distance to learn from them and forgive all involved, including yourself. Find refuge in your heart, which knows that suffering is *grace*.

8
MARCH

Loving-Kindness Meditation: Balance

Rest your attention in the feeling of the breath in the body. Then gently repeat these phrases:

May I live in balance.

May you live in balance.

May we live in balance.

Now notice how you feel. Repeat this practice throughout your day, whenever you feel yourself moving out of balance.

9
MARCH

Time to Water the Garden

When you catch yourself judging someone else, use it as a reminder to tend to some of the little broken pieces within yourself. The person you are judging is offering you a mirror. With the support of a deep breath, take this opportunity to wish yourself well.

10
MARCH

Inner Critic

Look around and notice people outwardly reacting to their inner critics. Notice people whispering insults to themselves, shaking their heads, or furrowing their brows. This is an opportunity to wish them the power to regain mindfulness. Make the same wish for yourself when you notice that you are reacting to your own inner critic.

11
MARCH

Align with What Works and Leave the Rest

How can you see clearly what holds you back? Start by examining your passions, thinking patterns, and emotional style.

What makes you feel alive? This should point you in the direction of your passions.

When you are lost in the fiction of your thoughts, what kinds of stories does your mind invent? Are they supportive, negative, fearful, insecure? These are your thinking patterns.

When you are feeling down, angry, or excited, how do you respond? Do you cope on your own, or do you connect with others? Do you lash out, hide, or maybe eat to handle your feelings? This is your emotional style.

Take a few moments to write down what comes to mind about your own passions, thinking patterns, and emotional style. Do you feel supported by them? Are they in alignment with your heart? Which are harmful? Which are healthy? What should you keep? What should you replace?

Take a deep breath and repeat to yourself: "I can cultivate healthy behaviors that are in alignment with my passions and my dreams. I release the behaviors and thinking patterns that hold me back from my passions and my dreams."

12
MARCH

Body Scan: Hips

Bring your awareness to the body and how it is making contact with your seat or the floor. Notice the sensations of touch and pressure as your body touches anything, including your clothes and the air. Take a few breaths.

Now focus your attention on the sensations of breathing. Stay aware of this breath and then the next breath, as it moves in and out of your body.

Now bring your attention to your hips, an area where emotions and trauma may be stored. Scan that area: Side hips, sitting bones, the space where your hips and thighs meet. Notice what sensations you're experiencing: Pressure, tightness, tingling, or anything else you notice. Visualize channeling your breath into your hips, releasing any tension you may be holding there. If you experience nothing, that is okay, too.

13

MARCH

Why Are You So Confused About Who You Are?

Confusion makes us feel like something is wrong with us, inviting the inner critic to become loud and obnoxious. The next time you feel confused, stop whatever you're doing and, with the support of the breath, ask the tough questions: What do I really want? What needs to change? Simply asking these questions helps us cultivate the courage that we need to go from confusion to clarity.

14
MARCH

Things Are Good

Don't allow the inner critic to question your peace or happiness. Sometimes life is simple and things feel light. Enjoy it! It doesn't mean you're not doing enough or that something might be wrong. Relax. Everything is good.

15
MARCH

You've Checked Out

When the inner critic is overreacting to life, it means that you have left the present moment and drifted into a faraway place. With the support of the breath, regain mindfulness of the present moment and match your attention with compassion.

16
MARCH

Who I'm Not Affirmation

"I'm not fearful. I'm not carrying a bag of guilt and grudges close to my heart. I'm not intentionally being mean and cynical to people around me. I'm not competing with anyone. I'm not working a lot to just accumulate stuff to show off. I'm not seeking anyone's approval. I'm not allowing my emotional letdowns to eat away at me. I'm not getting wasted because I can't cope with my wrongdoings. I'm not being vicious with my body. I'm not my past."

17
MARCH

Receiving Sound Meditation

Come into your meditation posture—at ease, yet alert. Allow your eyes to close or rest in a soft gaze a few feet in front of you.

Invite some relaxation by taking a few long breaths in and out and grounding yourself into this present moment.

When you are ready, open up your field of awareness to what sounds there are to be experienced in this moment. Allow yourself to just receive sound. Observe the quality of the sound, and observe how it passes away. See if you can just observe a sound without judging or criticizing it.

18
MARCH

Your Body Is Always in the Present

If you want to connect with the present moment,
reclaim mindfulness by connecting with your breath.

19
MARCH

Rewrite Fear with the Breath

Has this ever happened to you? You are walking home at night, and you see someone far off in the dark, crossing the street toward you. You wonder if the person is dangerous or intends to hurt you. Your mind gets agitated with worst-case scenarios. Your whole body becomes tense.

And then, as you get closer, you see that the person is an elderly man slowly making his way home. You had created a whole story in your mind, and the man had nothing to do with the stories you invented about him.

With the support of your breath, you can replace fear with calmness and meet the reality of any given situation with present-moment awareness instead of an invented story. Anytime your mind starts to wander into fiction, breathe and come back to the Now.

20
MARCH

Don't Miss the Invitation

Radical healing takes place when you can accept that the fear you're experiencing is an invitation to come into closer contact with courage.

21
MARCH

Reality Check

Underneath anxiety is fear. With the support of your breath, take a moment to ask yourself, "Is this fear based in reality or created by my imagination?" This simple question can break you out of the cycle of anxiety and strengthen your determination to be free.

22
MARCH

Worthiness Mantra

I am worth the effort; therefore,

I'm allowing myself to be forgiven,

I'm allowing myself to forgive,

I'm allowing myself to be healed,

I'm allowing myself to heal others,

I'm allowing myself to be loved,

I'm allowing myself to love.

And so it is.

And so it is.

And so it is!

23
MARCH
—

Your Alarm Clock Is Going Off

May all parts of yourself awaken to what is
already awake within you.

24
MARCH
—

Unlocking Your Treasure Affirmation

"I am here to open
everything that is locked
within me."

25
MARCH

—

Becoming a Vessel

Begin by feeling your breath in your body for two minutes.

Now visualize yourself just before you took shape, just before your birth—before hope, before fear, before all self-identification.

Breathing in, ask yourself: *Who am I?*

Breathing out: Allow the answers to come to you. Notice if the mind is clinging to labels or means of identifying yourself.

Breathing in, ask again: *Who am I?*

Breathing out: Allow the answers to come to you.

As you continue to breathe, continue to ask, "Who am I?" and allow the answers to come to you. Gradually allow the identifications and labels to fade away.

26
MARCH

—

Serenity, Are You There?

Practice the middle way, a balanced state of being from which you do your best—not in any extreme high or low, not perfect, not a failure, just your best. Enough. When you feel yourself veering off to one extreme or another, return to the middle, with the support of the breath, and regain equanimity.

27
MARCH

—

Kindness Affirmation

"Today I choose to be kinder to myself and everyone around me."

28
MARCH

The Spotlight Is On You

Practice turning the spotlight of your awareness away from the outside world and onto your internal landscape—the inner you. Check in with yourself. Notice what's present. Can you determine the quality of your thoughts? Perhaps there's a sticky thought playing out in a loop. Each time you remember to check in with your inner you, with an accepting and kind intention, the more you'll notice the sticky thoughts losing their power and passing by without disturbing you.

29
MARCH

Purpose Affirmation

"Today I feel certainty and purpose about who I am and what I'm doing."

30
MARCH

Dear Heart

Gently ask, "Dear heart, who am I?"
Allow the answer to come to you.

31
MARCH

Integration with the Breath

Breathing in, say: *I accept the broken pieces in me.*

Breathing out, say: *I accept that those parts of me have been the guiding force of my healing and growth.*

Breathing in: *I'm learning to hold in my heart all parts of me.*

Breathing out: *I accept my trauma as a part of the world's trauma.*

APRIL

———

COURAGE

1

Follow Your Deeper Wisdom

When someone gives you advice, you usually think before choosing whether or not to follow it, right? You might say yes when you feel like that advice resonates with your path, and you might say no because you know that it would not best suit you.

Practice applying the same principle with your thoughts and emotions: You can choose whether to take their advice or not. It's up to you!

2

Hit the "Like" Button

Sometimes you have to read the comments to remember your greatness. Sometimes you just have to not care what the comments say and just remind yourself of your greatness.

Inviting in Painful Memories

Painful memories have a way of showing up when you least expect them. When it happens, you can choose to look at the memories or distract yourself from them. Inviting in painful memories takes courage, but when you do it enough times, eventually you won't be afraid of the memories or triggered by them. By inviting them in, you take away their power and reclaim yours.

Regard Your Past as a Dream

Your past does not define who you are. Today, choose to make amends with all of your harmful past actions, and cultivate the strength to forgive yourself. You'll start seeing more clearly than ever before.

5
APRIL

Loving-Kindness Meditation: Bravery

Start by resting your attention in the feeling of the breath in the body. Then gently repeat these phrases:

May I be brave.

May you be brave.

May we be brave together.

Now notice how you feel. Repeat this practice throughout your day, whenever you feel that you need a bit of bravery.

6
APRIL

What Would You Create?

We can easily get caught up in a cycle of thinking like this: "If I didn't have to do x, then I would be doing y." What would you be able to create if you decided to let go of the x—if you let go of the inexhaustible list of excuses for staying stuck?

Would you compose a song or a poem? Would you write a story, make a painting, take a class, build something, try a new recipe, play an instrument, do an art project? What would you create?

Today, spend five minutes creating something you usually excuse away because you're too busy, too tired, too old, too inexperienced, too _____ (fill in the blank). See if you can build a new daily or weekly habit of engaging in the act of creation.

7

APRIL

A Letter for Your Future Self

Give your past self a shout-out for being brave enough to start again, for having the courage to cultivate the patience to heal, and for getting you to where you are right now. And to your future self, declare:

I'm committed.

I'm trusting.

I got this.

I got you!

8

APRIL

The Power of Your Presence

Take responsibility for the quality of your presence,
and remember that your presence alone can be healing.

9

APRIL

Courage Affirmation

I have the courage to ask for what I want.

I have the courage to speak my dreams into reality.

I have the courage to be fearless.

I have the courage to step fully into my transformation.

I have the courage to let go of people, habits, and things in my life that don't support my healing.

I have the courage to love myself so deeply that it inspires others to love themselves too.

I have the courage to be a new version of myself each day.

I have the courage to let go of my past.

I have the courage to be free.

10
APRIL

No Attachment Affirmation

"Today I will participate fully in my life and be unattached to the outcomes."

11
APRIL

Practice Tree Hugging

Standing with your feet hip-width apart, hold your arms out in front of your chest in a round shape, as if you were hugging a large tree.

Feel your feet rooted on the ground. Breathe into your abdomen, and focus your attention on that area of the body.

12
APRIL

Hey, You Over There!

The next time you observe fearful thoughts playing out in your mind, take a moment to greet them: "Hi, fearful thoughts." This process helps you remember that thoughts are mental events and nothing more.

Remember, you are not your thoughts, and you are not broken even if you often get caught in a fear-based mind-set. Consistently being vigilant of your internal landscape allows you to make a change.

13
APRIL

—

What's Your Accountant Got to Say?

Today, perform a self-inventory: What habits do you have that cultivate compassion, wonder, and beauty? And what habits do you have that cultivate anxiety, fear, and increased self-criticism?

Once you've written down or thought of at least three habits for each question, take the opportunity to notice which habits are working for you and leading you on a path of freedom, and which are keeping you stuck.

14
APRIL

—

Stop Scolding

There's no power in beating yourself up! Stop catastrophizing. If you notice that you're being self-critical, take a deep breath into your belly and say, "I accept myself."

15
APRIL

Beginner's Mind: Mindful Eating

As you sit down for a meal today, imagine you have just been dropped off from another planet and have never before seen what you are about to eat.

With a sense of wonder and a nonjudgmental curiosity, explore it, examine it, smell it.

Once you have spent some time examining the food, take the first bite.

As you do, notice the food going into your mouth. Feel the sensations around your teeth, tongue, the roof of the mouth. Feel the different tastes, temperatures, and textures.

Take your time with each bite, fully chewing and mindfully swallowing. Can you trace the food all the way down your throat to your stomach?

After you swallow, take a pause and a few breaths, noticing how you feel.

Gathering all of your attention, be one with your meal.

Allow yourself to *just* eat. No working or reading or looking at a device or talking or worrying or thinking about your next task. You are simply eating. Let eating be a meditation.

16
APRIL

Judgment Cleanse

Throughout the day, do your very best to not judge anyone or yourself—
not even once!

17
APRIL

When the Student Is Ready

Find teachers and a community that support your healing and growth. Place
yourself around people who inspire you. Nurture relationships with people
who support your movement toward the life you want and whom you want
to take into that life with you. As you make choices that lead you along your
path, trust that the people you need will find you.

18
APRIL

—

How Does It Feel to Be a Boss?

Rest your attention on the feeling of the breath in the body for a few moments.

In your mind's eye, recall an experience where you felt totally present and comfortable, confident and empowered.

Do your best to recall the details, using all of your senses: What you smelled, tasted, saw, heard, touched, and felt.

When you have a clear memory of the experience and how good you felt, think of a current event where you wish to feel just as confident. Allow the confident feeling from your past experience to permeate your visualization of the current experience. For a few moments, do your best to keep that self-confident, empowered feeling in the current experience visualization.

Then take a few breaths and notice how you feel in your body.

19
APRIL

I Approve of Me

You don't need approval from others. Approve of yourself. Your reason for doing anything is a good enough reason. Trust your choices.

20
APRIL

Miracles Affirmation

"I'm open to miracles."

21
APRIL

Affirmation for Healthy Eating

"Today I change my relationship to food. I choose foods that heal and energize my body."

22
APRIL

Your Personal Mission

Take responsibility for your life by owning the fact that you have chosen all of it, as hard as it might be to accept this fact. May you continue to learn from the lessons, and may you continue to rejoice in awe of all the blessings.

23
APRIL

Vitality Mantra Meditation

Breathing in, say: *I am*

Breathing out, say: *Healing.*

Breathing in: *I am*

Breathing out: *Vital and alive.*

Breathing in: *I am*

Breathing out: *Vibrant.*

Breathing in: *I am*

Breathing out: *Perfectly well.*

24
APRIL

Body Scan Meditation: The Neck

Take a comfortable seat, and allow a few long cleansing breaths to ground you.

Using your attention, start a scan of the back of your neck. Notice if there is smoothness, tingling, or tension. The neck is a place where we tend to hold tension. Allow whatever you notice to just be there. Closely feel the sensations inside your neck, the bottom of the skull, the sides of the neck, the front of the neck, the throat. Become aware of the life that is there.

25
APRIL

Resentment Cleanse

Take a moment to observe how many grudges you're holding on to.
With the support of your breath and an intention of acceptance, look
back at your interactions with others and notice if you're still carrying
bits of resentment about them. The same way you cleanse your body
daily, it's necessary to cleanse your mind of this fog of bitterness.
Otherwise, this unprocessed emotional baggage can show up
two-fold when you least expect it.

26
APRIL

Reminder

Self-acceptance is self-care.

27
APRIL

The Many Faces of Anger

Anger is often trapped fear expressing itself. It's much easier to be angry than to show vulnerability. Why are you angry? Another way to ask this is: What are you afraid of? Is it possible to forgive yourself for feeling angry, scared, and vulnerable? Take a moment to think of all the things you're angry about. Now, with compassion, forgive yourself for each one.

28

Can You Forgive?

Take a moment to reflect on how you handled mistakes as you were growing up. Were those around you hard on you? Did they make you feel ashamed? Were your mistakes judged, punished, or forgiven?

Now observe how you handle mistakes today. Is there a resemblance? Are you hard on yourself? Do you make yourself feel ashamed? Do you judge or punish yourself for your mistakes, or are you able to forgive yourself?

29
APRIL

Being Brave

Be brave enough to not let yourself be defined by one choice, one situation, or one result. You may contradict yourself at times. That's because you're not perfect, and because you're made of multitudes.

30
APRIL

Taking Things Personally

Observe your expectations. How much do you expect from others? How much of the disappointment you feel is a result of expectations that you have placed on others—expectations that they may know nothing about?

You may have a running list of things you expect others to know—things you believe are common sense. But we are all different. What's common sense for one person is foreign to another. Observe your expectations. Which ones are appropriate, and which ones are not?

Express your needs that are based in truth, and release those that aren't, with the understanding that they were past or future projections of the mind, not present-moment reality. Now has no expectation.

PART TWO

Worth It

MAY

PEACE

1
MAY

—

Beyond Thoughts

When you enter the present moment, you have access to a realm beyond thoughts, where beauty, creativity, joy, and inner peace arise.

2
MAY

—

Back to Center

Cultivate the habit of balance. Notice when you're carried away from your center by extremes of rage or excitement. With the support of the breath, come back to your balanced middle point.

3

MAY

Abundance Invocation

Ask yourself, "What does abundance mean to *me?*" Allow the answer to come to you.

Now repeat to yourself three times, "I believe I am worthy of having abundance."

Now imagine that you are walking in a forest. Your feet are bare, and you can feel the cool breeze of the forest and the wet grass underneath your feet. As you continue walking, notice that the trees are closer and closer to each other, and leaves are brushing your arms.

Then you notice that you've entered a clearing in the forest. Take a moment to twirl around in this clearing. As you come to a slow stop, you notice that all the abundance you've imagined for yourself is all around you. That abundance could include friends, money, a partner. Whatever it includes, you're surrounded by it. Be there with all of it.

Now repeat to yourself three times, "Because I can imagine this abundance, it is possible for it to be my reality, and I am worthy of it all."

4
MAY

What Makes You Feel Alive?

In moments of peace, joy, flow—moments of doing what makes you feel alive—you are reminded of who you truly are.

5
MAY

Stay Present with Yourself

Self-love is not allowing yourself to get lost in imagining what others think of you.

6
MAY

Loving-Kindness Meditation: Forgiveness

Start by resting your attention in the feeling of the breath in the body. Then gently repeat these phrases:

May I learn to forgive myself.
May you learn to forgive yourself.
May we learn to forgive ourselves.

Now notice how you feel. Repeat this meditation throughout your day, especially if you find yourself feeling judgment toward yourself or another.

7
MAY

Thoughts Are Just Thoughts

Throughout the day, remind yourself that thoughts are passing before you, not originating from you.

8
MAY

True Companionship

When the mind, heart, and body are in alignment,
you're not alone.

9
MAY

Welcome Home

Dear blessed one,

I want you to know that here you are welcome. Here you belong.
Here you are enough. Welcome home!

Sincerely,

Your heart

10
MAY

Discernment

Self-love is knowing that although certain things may feel good, they are not necessarily good for you.

11
MAY

Respond with the Inner Wise Teacher

Have you noticed that sometimes when you allow your thoughts alone to react to life, you might miss an opportunity to connect more deeply? This is because your thoughts might be dense with and informed by impatience. And when you allow your emotions alone to react to life, you can go into a downward spiral, because your feelings might be charged with unconscious anger or frustration.

Instead of responding with just thoughts or emotions, take a deep breath and find your heart, your inner wise teacher, and respond to life from there.

12
MAY

Real Happiness

Happiness is the ability to maintain your equanimity as you ride along in the human experience, despite all its emotional ups and downs; to choose to be proactive instead of reactive; and to practice compassion and kindness as your default.

13
MAY

The Real You Is Right Now

You can only know who you are when you are in the present moment.

14
MAY

Body Scan Meditation: The Head

This is a practice for focusing your attention on the sensory experiences in your head. It will shift your attention away from the thinking mind and into the felt sensation of this area of the body.

Find a place to sit. Find stillness in yourself and welcome a few deep breaths to ground yourself and arrive in the present moment.

Start to feel your body from the inside out. Take a few moments to scan your body, bringing presence and relaxation to it. Notice where your breath is present in your body right now.

Bring your attention to the top of your head. Slowly scan your hairline and forehead, releasing any tension you may be holding on to.

Relax the muscles around your eyes. Notice the eyelids resting over the eyeballs.

Bring your attention to your cheekbones and jaw. Just observe the sensations in those areas.

Now move your awareness to the back of the head, then the skull, and then the scalp. Bring your attention to the inside of the skull. Just explore what there is to be experienced. Simply notice.

15
MAY

—

Worthiness Affirmation

"I am present, and I am enough."

16
MAY

—

Accidentally Creating
the Life You Don't Want

Notice how much time you spend visualizing worst-case scenarios in your mind—a variety of situations that you never really want to see happen. Notice when you've been swept up and drifted into this land of catastrophe. And take a moment to acknowledge that the vast majority of these scenarios never happen.

17
MAY

Infinite Patience Meditation

Breathing in, say: *I have patience.*

Breathing out, say: *I am learning to trust the process.*

Breathing in: *I am not worried.*

Breathing out: *I wait like a lover.*

Breathing in: *I wait blissfully.*

Breathing out: *I wait ecstatically.*

Breathing in: *I wait gracefully.*

Breathing out: *I cherish this moment in its totality.*

Breathing in: *I explore this moment with acceptance.*

Breathing out: *I am not rushing for tomorrow.*

18
MAY

Inviting Clarity

Visualize yourself experiencing clarity in everything you do today.

19
MAY

Freedom from Mental Constructs

Observe everything around you: Your notebook, coffeemaker, laptop, mirror, alarm clock, even your thoughts and feelings. Notice the meaning you have attached to them. This essentialist viewpoint keeps you stuck, because in reality, nothing outside of your heart has an inherent essential nature; it's all a mental construct.

Today, practice seeing the objects in your surrounding as just objects—nothing more. Practice seeing your thoughts and feelings as just thoughts and feelings—nothing more.

20
MAY

How to Use Memories to Be More Present

Everyone has both blissful and painful memories. Unless you train your mind to have a new relationship with them, you'll continue to be dragged away by the painful ones or to desperately crave the blissful ones.

Next time you find yourself carried away with a memory, take a breath, anchor yourself in the present moment, and creatively ignore it by repeating a phrase that empowers you. With time, you will become better at reframing these memories when they arise, and you will remember that you can't be in the past and in the present at the same time.

21
MAY

Redefining Survival

Self-love is survival.

Forgiveness is survival.

Healing is survival.

Starting over is survival.

Transformation is survival.

Dreaming big is survival.

Unconditional love is survival.

22
MAY

Be Present for Peace

The more people live in the present moment, the less conflict there will be.

23
MAY

Revising Stories of Pain

Birth, aging, sickness, and death are usually seen as painful parts of the human experience. If you choose to observe these moments as objectively as possible and not let yourself get carried away by the stories the mind fabricates about their painfulness, you're contributing to a different future.

24
MAY

Talking to the Inner Critic

Grab a pen and paper. Listen in on your inner critic. What's it saying?
Take a few moments to write down the negative self-talk you witness
and then read it out loud. Notice how absurd it is, how cruel. You would
never speak to your best friend in this way. Today, change the script
and talk to yourself like you are your own best friend.

25
MAY

What Is Yours

Today, practice noticing the quality of your feelings and thoughts
when you're around people.

If you observe that the quality of your internal landscape around
certain people becomes negative and sticky, use the support of your
breath to reclaim your power to separate what's yours and what could
be their projections.

26
MAY

Attuning with the Heart

When you allow yourself to see beauty in others, flaws and all, you're deconditioning your mind from seeing ugliness. Each time this process takes place, you're attuning with the heart's language.

27
MAY

Be Willing to Be Surprised

How open and willing are you to allow a completely new turn of events to unfold today? For today, practice harmonizing your mind with the wonder of the heart.

28
MAY

Saying Grace

As you sit down to eat today, take a moment to close your eyes and set an intention: "Thank you everyone everywhere who created the conditions for me to have this food. May this food nourish and heal me. May this food fill me with energy to continue to carry out my mission. I wish for all beings everywhere to have the nourishment they need."

29
MAY

Morning Check-in

When you wake up, observe if you're already giving yourself a hard time. Notice what feelings are present and the tone of the inner monologue. If you notice that the quality of your internal landscape is unpleasant, take the opportunity to shift your attention to someone else and how you can help someone feel better today.

30
MAY

Inner Calm Visualization

Take a moment to visualize what your life would look like if you could free yourself of internal chaos. How would you be feeling? Where would you be? What would you be doing? Who is around you?

31
MAY

Mantra Meditation: I Am Willing to Heal

For the next few moments, rest your attention on this phrase: "I am willing to heal." Repeat it in your mind. This is your meditation. If at any moment during your meditation your mind becomes distracted, kindly and gently come back to the mantra. Each time you repeat the mantra with presence and grace, you're breaking your subtle cycles of helplessness, being a victim of your experience, and fear of changing.

JUNE

———

CHANGE

1

Garden of Opposites

On the other side of impatience is patience. On the other side of neglecting is nurturing. On the other side of busy is calm. On the other side of controlling is allowing. You have the ability to choose which qualities are most present throughout your day. Each choice plants a seed for the next choice.

2

JUNE

Attachments Lead to Suffering

You have a choice to make each day: To cultivate a relationship with your attachments or your happiness. Each time you make a choice to deepen your relationship with happiness, you learn to hang out with your attachments in a less entangled way.

3

Visualizing Change

One day you wake up and notice that your beliefs have changed. The way you see yourself and the world has changed. You believe in something new, something more integrated, something more liberating, something closer to your heart. At that moment you may laugh out loud, and you may think, "Wow, how long have I been carrying around the old ways? Why didn't I know this before?" Have gratitude for everything and everyone that got you to this point.

4
JUNE

Body Scan Meditation: Throat

Purse your lips as if you had a straw in your mouth, and breathe in deeply. Then breathe out through your nose. Now gather all of your attention and rest it on your throat, the point of communication in the body. For the next few moments, feel the breath passing by the back of your throat.

This practice helps you become more conscious of how you speak and strengthens your ability to speak clearly and compassionately to yourself and the world.

5
JUNE

The Relationship of Feelings and Thoughts

When you notice your current relationship with your feelings, you can change your thoughts, and if you can change your thoughts, you can change how you feel.

6
JUNE

Heed the Signals

Triggers are messengers signaling the parts of you that still need healing. With the support of your breath, look inside for how to heal these parts.

7
JUNE

It's Not That Bad

When things are bad, take a breath and notice the tendency to start believing things to be far worse than they actually are. Each time you remember to come back to the breath, you disrupt the default mind-set of creating worst-case scenarios. With this practice, you're training your mind to respond skillfully (instead of simply reacting) to the situation at hand.

8

Noticing the Habits of the Mind

Do you always assume the worst? Do you get stressed out easily? Do you think there is never enough time in the day? Do you feel that your relationships are draining? Do you wake up at night because your mind won't stop overthinking? Do you frequently find that you can't sit still? Do you feel tired and sick often?

Did you say yes to half of these questions? If so, you've probably realized that this is no way to live. It's time to stop practicing the things you don't want to become your reality.

9
JUNE

A Part of Me Is Angry

When anger strikes, it's important to recognize that only a part of you is experiencing anger. Start by saying, "A part of me feels angry." This vocabulary choice helps you objectively listen to other parts of you that are not experiencing anger.

10
JUNE

Less Destruction

If you want to be fully alive, you must learn to work with your painful memories and negative thoughts, otherwise you will be trapped by them. When one of these memories or thoughts arises, combat it with an empowering thought right away, to keep it from leading to more destructive thoughts.

11
JUNE

Expired Stories

For one moment, see if you can shift your perspective of a painful memory—even by just an inch. Can you be open to the possibility that your interpretation of what happened is the by-product of hurt feelings? Your misinterpretation could be causing you to add layers of guilt to the unpleasant memory again and again each time it comes up. Recognizing that your interpretation is just that—one personal, subjective interpretation—doesn't take away from what happened, but makes you aware of all the layers that have been added to the memory over the years.

12
JUNE

Upgrade Feelings of Comparison

When you notice that you're hooked in a downward spiral of comparison, use it as a portal to help you access and exercise compassion for yourself and all beings.

13
JUNE

Time for a Dip

Yesterday is a projection of the mind—memories of past events. Tomorrow is also a projection of the mind—fantasies of events that haven't yet happened. Yesterday and tomorrow offer us opportunities to dwell in anxiety, fear, and insecurity.

The present moment offers the opposite: Reality and radical acceptance. Reality is now. Reality is deep acceptance. When you sustain your attention in the present moment, a deep peace flushes away doubt and fear.

Today, pay attention to when your mind starts revisiting yesterday or imagining tomorrow. When it does, come back and take a dip in the peaceful waters of the Now.

When you feel yourself dwelling in thoughts of yesterday or tomorrow—such as how you misspoke or an event you fear will go badly—gently anchor yourself back into the present moment. Each time you do, you're training your mind to have a longer present-moment attention span and fewer detours into past and future projections. You can train your mind to make this place of peace and acceptance your default.

14
JUNE

Practice Love

Studying love does not heal. Sharing love is what heals.

15
JUNE

On Lust

You know your meditation practice is working when you can hang out with your cravings in a gentle way. You're able to observe the itch arising, but you choose to not compulsively act on it.

16
JUNE

You Are the Medicine

Find a way to be available to yourself. You are the mantra, the meditation, and the remedy.

17
JUNE

Moments Change Everything

Each moment is an opportunity to be liberated from fixed identities you hold for yourself and others.

18
JUNE

Mentor Bonding Meditation

Bring to your mind an image of a teacher—someone who has inspired you, who has helped you from far away or nearby. Say their name to yourself, to get a feel for their presence, strength, integrity, and confidence. Now visualize these qualities being passed on to you as a teacher-to-student transmission. Repeat in your mind, "I want to have these qualities within me."

19
JUNE

Loving-Kindness Meditation: Truth

Rest your attention on the feeling of the breath in the body. Then gently repeat the following phrases:

May I learn to speak the truth.

May you learn to speak the truth.

May we learn to speak the truth.

Now notice how you feel. Repeat this meditation throughout your day, especially at times when you sense a reluctance to be fully honest with yourself or others.

20
JUNE

Affirmation for Painful Memories

"Today I allow myself to purge painful memories. Today I notice that voice of suffering pulling me away from my potential to live, laugh, and love."

21
JUNE

Watching the Same Movie

Unless you stop the domino effect of your emotions,
your life is on repeat.

22
JUNE

Who You Are Is Enough

Sometimes we spend a lot of time trying to predict what other people think of us—and most of our predictions are wrong. It's time to trust that who you are is good enough and that you cannot control how others are going to perceive you. Trust that your intentions are pure and that you are doing your best.

23
JUNE

Mantra Meditation: I Am Worthy

I am worthy of a life free from anxious thoughts that take up space in my mind.

I am worthy of the freedom to be me.

I am worthy of shining bright.

I am worthy of being good.

I am worthy of changing my habits for ones that are healthy.

I am worthy of feeling energized.

I am worthy of not repeating the same mistakes.

I am worthy of doing work that I love.

I am worthy of abundance.

I am worthy of waking up each day excited and curious.

I am worth the effort!

24
JUNE

Reviewing Your Toolkit

Take notice of what's in your mental toolkit: Do you have reliable tools to help you meet life with less fear and anxiety, and with more love and forgiveness? Take this opportunity to empty your toolkit and only keep things that serve you.

25
JUNE

Blessed Be the Unseen You

Take time to nurture the parts of you that you can't see.

26
JUNE

—

Affirmation for Times of Difficulty

"Even though I am experiencing difficulty, today I choose to connect to the inner part of myself that doesn't experience difficulty. Today I choose to express myself from that part."

27
JUNE

Body Scan Meditation: Sleep

This body scan meditation will help you prepare for sleep.

Lie down comfortably on your bed, and bring your attention to your breath. Take a few breaths to land in this moment, moving out of the thinking mind and into the body.

Start to feel your body against the bed. Notice any sensations of heaviness, tingling, pressure, movement, or heat. Just notice these or any other sensations without trying to change them.

Now scan the body. Begin at the top of the head. Move to the back of the head, down your face, to the jawline, the back of the neck, the throat, the clavicle area. If you notice the mind has snagged on a thought or been distracted by a sound, just bring it back to the most recent part of the body with compassion and ease.

Continue moving your attention to your chest and abdomen and then to the upper back, middle back, and lower back. You might notice new sensations, and that is okay. Allow any sensations to come and go.

Continued

Move to the arms, hands, fingers. Move to your hips, allowing each to soften as you continue to breathe. Move now to your legs. Maybe there is itching, tingling, or other sensations. Whatever there is, let it be. Continuing to breathe, move to the knees, calves, ankles, both feet, and all ten toes.

Breathing in, say in your mind: "I am resting." Breathing out, say in your mind: "I am relaxing. I am allowing my body to rest and relax."

28
JUNE

Your Dialogue with Yourself

Notice the thinking that is a back and forth between you and you.

29
JUNE

Alignment Affirmation

"Today my intentions match my speech and my actions."

30
JUNE

The Truth Is Always Available

The more you come in close contact with each moment, the more the emotional charge of painful memories will dissipate, allowing you to notice the additional stories that were fabricated by your mind and how far from the truth you've been.

JULY

———

GROWTH

1

Being in the Flow

How often do you experience flow but disregard it or take it for granted? These are moments of symbiotic communication with life, of total integration, when we are immersed in the present so deeply that we become one with everything. These moments are more powerfully experienced rather than explained. These are moments of wholeness and inner peace. May you continue to create the conditions to experience more of these moments and the magic they have to offer.

2

JULY

Things in Flow Affirmation

"Today I take a moment to memorize how it feels when things are in flow."

3
JULY

Loving-Kindness Meditation: Humanness

Rest your attention in the feeling of the breath in the body. Then gently repeat these phrases:

May I learn to embrace my humanness.

May you learn to embrace your humanness.

May we learn to embrace our humanness.

Now notice how you feel. Repeat this meditation practice throughout your day to gently remind yourself of our common humanity.

4
JULY

Moments of Grace

Observe the next time the inner critic is quiet. You feel present and are not longing to be elsewhere. There are fewer thoughts, and there is ease within—almost as if everything were happening in slow motion. These are your moments of grace.

5
JULY

Storytelling

Today, practice sharing an untold part of your story. Doing so will serve as a reminder of our shared human conditioning, and it can set you free. Then ask someone to share an untold part of their story with you. While listening, do your best to rest your alert attention on each word.

6

Body Scan Meditation: Hands

Find a comfortable position with your palms facing up. Gather all of your attention into your left hand. Feel the pulsing sensation in your hand. Become intimate with everything that is happening in your hand. If you notice that you are starting to create a story about what you're feeling or sensing, just invite your attention back to what you are experiencing in your left hand.

Now open your attention to both hands, left and right, and hold it there. Which hand do you use to receive? Which hand do you use to create? Notice the powers of each of your hands.

7
JULY

Ask and Receive

Take out a notebook and a pen. Take three long deep breaths to land back in your body.

Now read the following questions and mindfully journal your answers. Be as imaginative and honest as you can with your answers:

What do I need from the world to feel supported?

How do I want to transform in my personal evolution?

What qualities do I want to possess?

What do I want to give back?

What impact do I want to have in the world?

What can I do today?

8
JULY

Present Moment Affirmation

"Today I gently and kindly resist the temptation to get carried away by thoughts, especially negative ones, and I choose to return my attention to the present moment."

9
JULY

Light the Way

By sharing your truth with others, with honesty and vulnerability, you inspire your family, your friends, and each person you encounter to speak from their hearts with love and compassion. By speaking truth from the heart, you grant others permission to do the same.

10
JULY

Take a Risk

Ask yourself what you want to do but haven't done because that voice in your head holds you back. Today, take a risk and go there. You're worth the effort!

11
JULY

What Is Your Story?

Life is responding to the stories you tell about yourself.

12
JULY

New Experience Affirmation

"Today I remind myself that I do not have to experience life the way I was told."

13
JULY

Sitting by a Waterfall

Imagine yourself sitting by a waterfall. Feel yourself breathing in and breathing out. Feel yourself connected to nature, and allow the sounds of flowing water to calm your mind and release tension from your body. Visualize yourself feeling totally refreshed and energized.

14
JULY

No Mistakes

As often as you can, remind yourself that there's a reason for everything.

15
JULY

Give Thanks

Give thanks to the pain that gave you understanding and transformed you into who you are right now.

16
JULY

Acceptance Affirmation

"I'm learning each day to be okay with where I am. I trust where I'm going."

17
JULY

Equanimity

How do you enjoy the experience of excitement without becoming distracted? How can you become aware of anger without becoming destructive? How do you invite calmness without becoming passive?

18
JULY

We Are Just Passing By

Befriend the idea of death. Savor the Now, and give thanks for it all, because this won't last forever.

19
JULY

Mantra Meditation: I Am Worthy

Breathing in, say: *I am worth the effort.*

Breathing out, say: *I am allowing myself to heal.*

Breathing in: *I am worth the effort.*

Breathing out: *I am allowing myself to forgive.*

Breathing in: *I am worth the effort.*

Breathing out: *I am allowing myself to let go.*

Breathing in: *I am worth the effort.*

Breathing out: *I am allowing myself to love.*

Breathing in: *I am worth the effort.*

Breathing out: *I am allowing myself to be loved.*

Breathing in: *I am worth the effort.*

Breathing out: *I am allowing myself to shine.*

20
JULY

Break the Cycle

Stop recycling your traumas from childhood.

21
JULY

Affirmation for Change

"Today I will think differently.
Today I will emote differently.
Today I will behave differently."

22
JULY

—

Personality that Heals

Write down three of your positive characteristics and three of someone with whom you regularly interact.

23
JULY

—

The Space to Make a Choice

Feelings manifest first, and then arise thoughts charged with a craving for the good feelings or an aversion to the negative feelings. Become mindful of the space between feelings and thoughts, and from there, make a conscious choice.

24
JULY

Genuine Expression

Practice looking into the eyes of the person to whom you are expressing gratitude.

25
JULY

Compassion Affirmation

"Today, when empathy arises, I will respond with compassion."

26
JULY

What's Yours

Notice when you have diagnosed yourself with the feelings and thoughts of other people. With the support of your breath, wish yourself and others well. This way, you're letting go of what doesn't serve you and what isn't yours.

27
JULY

Private vs. Public

Practice noticing if your speech and actions are kind when you're around other people. Then notice if you use the same kind speech and actions with yourself when you're alone.

28
JULY

The Power of Peaceful Presence

There comes a moment when your presence alone makes everyone around you feel safe.

29
JULY

Quick Fix

Let the breath guide you. Solutions are just one breath away.

30
JULY

Your Mission

Listen to the sound of your mission, even though it might sound like pain at first.

31
JULY

Remember Your Flexibility

Re-centering is always possible. Practice noticing your opportunities to do so.

AUGUST
—
HEALING

1
AUGUST

—

What Do You Feed Your Mind?

If you serve yourself gratitude, kindness, and acceptance every day, your mind can reconnect you with your heart. But if you serve yourself negative self-talk, your mind will keep you trapped far away from the truth of your heart.

2
AUGUST

—

Identity Affirmation

"Today I let go of the false identities I have assumed for myself and others."

3

Body Scan Meditation: Feet

Relaxation is a full-body experience. Lie down with your arms by your side, palms facing up. Allow your body to feel supported by the earth beneath you.

Bring your attention to your feet. They do so much for you, getting you from one place to another. Bring your attention to your left foot. Feel the weight of your foot on the ground. Bring your attention to the ball of your foot, to the inner arch, to the outer edge as it touches the ground, to the heel, to your big toe and all of your other toes. Then to the right foot, noticing any differences. Feel the weight of your foot on the ground. Bring your attention to the ball of your foot, to the inner arch, to the outer edge as it touches the ground, to the heel, to your big toe and all of your other toes. Take this opportunity to rejoice in the freedom your feet provide you.

4

AUGUST

Receive Love and Goodwill

For one moment, imagine everyone around you wishing you well and sending you love. If you can visualize this, it is possible for it to become your reality.

5

AUGUST

Hide and Seek

If you want love to find you, stop hiding who you are. Practice meeting others with humility and showing up with all you've got.

6

AUGUST

Emotions Are Energy in Motion

When you are experiencing a negative emotion, become aware of where it lives in your body. With the support of your breath, hold space for the feeling in your body, gently closing your attention in on that feeling and letting thoughts fall to the background. When you hold space for the feeling in the body, it will run its course and dissipate.

7

AUGUST

When Am I Performing?

There are certain people in your life who can only hang out with your masks—not with your truth, not with your silence. They require you to constantly perform a role that suits their addiction to suffering. Notice when you're starting to perform the role that they expect of you.

8
AUGUST

Visualization: Flourishing

Visualize yourself filled with energy, vitality, and grace. Your body is self-healing and filled with potential. Visualize your whole body healthy, vibrant, and alive.

9
AUGUST

Your Business Card

Your presence introduces you before you even speak. Observe how it is introducing you.

10

Emotional Rebound

The only way to overcome negative emotions is to experience them. When you allow yourself to be with an experience without adding judgment or rushing to change your emotional state or feel a different way, over time you strip emotion of its power over you.

Bring your attention now to any negative emotion you may be experiencing. Take a deep breath in and out. What feelings are present? Stay with the feeling for a few more breaths. Experience the sensations associated with the emotion, observe the chatter and commentary your mind has to say about the experience. Now, with a newfound distance, release the emotion, the experience, and the thoughts.

Feelings arise; it is part of our human experience. Often they arise as a reminder that a part of you needs healing and only when you allow them can you tend to those parts of yourself. Suppressed emotions only come back twofold, so avoid running from them. It is possible to be in the presence of feelings without being ruled by them.

11

—

The Reserve

Have you realized that it feels better to be optimistic, to appreciate more and complain less? Optimism and appreciation constantly replenish your internal energy bank. When you cultivate a habit of optimism and appreciation, they become your default mind-set, and you live a better life. Practice noticing how you use your energy: Are you using it to complain or to appreciate?

12
AUGUST

Choose Which Inner Voices You Listen To

Take a moment to notice the main voices playing in your mind. Are they based on grief, anger, resentment, and sadness? For this moment, don't worry about why these voices are constantly playing in your mind. Rather, practice creatively ignoring the negative ones as they arise and continually choosing the positive ones—voices that are based on joy, gratitude, serenity, interest, hope, inspiration, awe, and love. With time, practice, and self-compassion, the negative voices will lose their power.

13
AUGUST

You Are the Miracle

Everything you need is within you now.

14
AUGUST

Show Me Your Greatness

Today, observe when you start to feel small and insecure. With the support of your breath, roll your shoulders round and back, feel your chest open and lift, and remember to take up space. Be bold, be bright, be powerful. It's your right to take up space just like that.

15

The View from the Penthouse

Have you ever gotten stuck in an old memory? Maybe you're ruminating about something you said and wondering if others are judging you for it. Perhaps you're feeling regret about something that already happened and that you cannot change.

Whatever it is, be open to the idea that perhaps you have only a limited view of the situation. Open your lens, even if it's just a tiny bit at a time, from a narrow to a panoramic perspective. Can you see any differences from this new view?

16

AUGUST

Your Innate Capacity

No trauma is too big to heal. We all have the capacity to heal trauma and live more peaceful and calm lives.

17
AUGUST

Self-Compassion

Where do you need healing? In which areas of your life do you still find tension and discomfort? Can you expand your field of compassion to those areas?

18
AUGUST

Not by Chance

You are carefully designing the person you are right now. It's time to take ownership of that creative process. You have chosen all of it thus far—the good, the challenging, the struggle, the beauty, and even the ugly. Life did not just happen. Life doesn't just happen. Just as you have made all the choices that led to this moment, you are now making the daring choice to heal and choose differently.

19
AUGUST

Rewriting Fearful Memories

You rewrite memory each time you remember it. So practice recalling memories from a place of nurturing and acceptance, thus disconnecting your memory from negative feelings.

20
AUGUST

Neutralizing Sadness

Meditate on sadness. Be with sadness. Experience how it makes you feel.

Notice how it changes the quality of your breath. Notice how your body responds to it.

Observe the sadness as a separate entity, using the breath to anchor yourself back into your body, back into the present moment. This makes sadness less unpleasant. The feeling of sadness becomes neutral.

21
AUGUST

—

No Strings Attached

Today, practice generosity—selfless giving with no strings attached and no expectation of thanks or reciprocation.

22
AUGUST

—

Insight

Rejoice in experiencing reality as it is. The freedom that comes from doing so clears delusion and allows you to see the difference between what is beneficial and what is harmful to yourself and others.

23
AUGUST

Integrity

Today, commit to speaking only the truth and keeping your promises.

24
AUGUST

Come Alive Meditation

Imagine what your life would look like if you were pursuing what makes you come alive. Start this visualization from the inside out: Hear a supportive, uplifting, and kind inner monologue. See that your posture is upright and confident; you carry yourself with grace and a gentle smile on your face. Your body is energized. You speak of creative ideas, and you compliment others around you. You have an abundance of love, and you support everyone around you.

25

AUGUST

Stories of Pain

How do you deal with pain in the body? Observe the stories you tell yourself about the physical sensations. Do these stories add to the pain, or do they add to your healing?

26

AUGUST

Secret Portals

By sitting in the middle of your internal chaos, you can learn from the portals that emotions open for you. These portals allow you to see that obstacles always come with a blessing.

27

AUGUST

Loving-Kindness Meditation: Healing

Start by resting your attention on the feeling of the breath in the body. Then gently repeat these phrases:

May I be healed.

May you be healed.

May we be healed.

Now notice how you feel. Use this meditation in creative ways throughout your day.

28
AUGUST

Resilience

Life's highs and lows can scar you deeply enough to make you not want to trust yourself or take any more risks. With the practice of meditation comes self-compassion, healing, and forgiveness, reminding you of your ability to rise with grace every time you fall.

29
AUGUST

Stealth Blessings

Give everyone you come in contact with today a silent blessing, wishing them healing and growth.

30
AUGUST

Even Your Toothbrush

Full participation with life means having gratitude for even the most ordinary things.

31
AUGUST

New Possibilities Affirmation

"I see opportunity and love even in the most broken pieces."

PART THREE

Freedom

SEPTEMBER

INTEGRATION

1
SEPTEMBER

Happiness Cannot Be Found Outside of Yourself

Society, our families, and culture tell us that if we had a better job, if we were prettier, if we were smarter, we would be happy. They don't remind us of the magic we carry within us; they don't tell us that this magic is the elixir that makes everlasting happiness, because they have forgotten. But thankfully, we have each other as reminders.

2
SEPTEMBER

The Power of the Practice

Meditation increases our inherent qualities of beauty, goodness, and compassion. And it decreases negative feelings. Do the work.

3

Loving-Kindness Meditation: Insight

Start by resting your attention on the feeling of the breath in the body. Then gently repeat these phrases:

May I become insightful.

May you become insightful.

May we become insightful for the benefit of all.

Now notice how you feel. Repeat this meditation throughout your day.

4

SEPTEMBER

Genuine Compassion

You have to feel genuine compassion for your own suffering in order to heal yourself and others.

5

Following Curiosity

Value your curiosities instead of judging them. Value them so much that you seek to learn more from them. Your curiosities are your heart asking to be discovered, your mission asking to come to life, your passion asking to manifest. They reflect an intelligence beyond anything that you have ever experienced.

6

Both Student and Teacher

Every day you are both the teacher and the student. With each person you encounter, you are learning or teaching. These experiences reflect what you need at that moment. Recognize when you are being called to listen and absorb knowledge, and when you are being called to share and affirm it.

7
SEPTEMBER

How Present Am I?

Portions of enlightenment are always available when you're present.

8
SEPTEMBER

Being of Service Affirmation

"Today I will ask for help when I need it, and I will help when I can."

9
SEPTEMBER

—

The Limits of Language

Language can't explain the essence of reality. Language is limited, and our essence is unlimited. Because the mind can't grasp something beyond language, it cannot grasp our essence. Only with our hearts can we experience our essence.

10
SEPTEMBER

—

Body Scan: Knees

Take a comfortable seat on a chair, on the floor, or on a meditation cushion. Rest your attention on the feelings of the breath in your body. Then gently move your attention to your knees. Start with your kneecaps, then move your attention to the area behind the knees, the inner knees, the outsides of the knees, the right knee, and the left knee. Notice the area where the knees and thighs meet, then notice the area where the knees and calves meet. Take a moment to reflect on how much your knees do for you every day.

11
SEPTEMBER

Attunement

Check in with your motives regularly: Do they lead to fulfillment?
Do they lead to healing? Do they hurt anyone?

12
SEPTEMBER

Embrace Everything

Learn to hold in your heart all the parts of your life. Doing so will help
inform your responses to the world with the most clear understanding.

13
SEPTEMBER

Real, but Not True

When you're suffering, the hurt may be a filter through which you perceive the world, and you may begin to project negativity into the world. With the support of your breath, you can notice the added filter and keep yourself from projecting the negativity you see through it onto the truth of the world.

14
SEPTEMBER

Beyond the Stories Affirmation

"Today I am devoted to helping myself remember who I truly am."

15
SEPTEMBER

Defusing Emotions

Emotions are energy combined with thoughts in motion. Instead of allowing yourself to get carried away in a downward spiral of negativity, you can stop the spiral of stories playing in your mind. With the support of the breath, bring your attention to the physical sensation of the emotion behind the stories and simply allow it to run its course.

16
SEPTEMBER

Be the Lighthouse

Your devotion to knowing yourself will make everyone around you feel like there's something special in them, too.

17

Equanimity

Today, observe your capacity to accept things with an inner poise
that cannot be upset by gain or loss.

18
SEPTEMBER

Wakeup Call

Sometimes the little things don't get you back into your body and back
in touch with reality. Sometimes something jarring has to happen to
bring you back.

19
SEPTEMBER

The Truth

Hang with those who seek the truth; don't hang with those who claim to have found it.

20
SEPTEMBER

Update the Programming

Notice how sometimes you don't know what to do, so you react based on your prejudice, which keeps you trapped in fearful ways. With practice, you can tune in to an intelligence beyond your conditioning and live proactively.

21
SEPTEMBER

Stay Curious

Sometimes all you've got are the questions you're asking.

22
SEPTEMBER

Become Aware of Your Emotional Habits

Blocking emotions and exaggerating emotions are one and the same.

23
SEPTEMBER

Part of the Puzzle

Remember, you play a fundamental role in the human family.

24
SEPTEMBER

Notice Your Priorities

What was essential is no longer essential.

25
SEPTEMBER

The Promise of More Bliss

Pleasure is always short-lived. Seeking pleasure alone
leaves us constantly dissatisfied.

26
SEPTEMBER

Widen Your View

Practice zooming out from your personal experience and into a wider view
of understanding and sharing in the experience of other people.

27
SEPTEMBER

What Keeps You Together

Find a comfortable seat. Feel your feet on the ground and your spine long and relaxed. Feel your body fill up with your presence.

Close your eyes and take a few breaths in and out, letting the breath lift up your posture. Feel your ribs expanding and contracting. Allow yourself to be just as you are.

As you breathe in, imagine your inhale starting at the bottom of your spine and traveling up to the top of your head. And as you breathe out, the breath sweeps down from the top of your head to the bottom of your spine.

Bring your attention to your spine. Send it gratitude for all it does for you, for how strong and powerful it is.

Rest in the feelings that arise from this practice and then open your eyes.

28
SEPTEMBER

Scrutiny

With practice, you learn to discern which feelings are guides
to listen to and which feelings are fake news.

29
SEPTEMBER

Learn to Swim

Come close to feelings, but don't drown in them.

30
SEPTEMBER

Life's Work Affirmation

"As I breathe in,
I come in closer contact
with my mission.
As I breathe out, I let go
of the self-sabotaging
mechanisms that were
once hardwired in me."

OCTOBER

FORGIVENESS

1
OCTOBER

Available Love

The love that is available to you is not limited to the love you know or the love that conditioned you. The love available to you is limitless.

2
OCTOBER

Step Back from Your Inner Noise

Often, we get swept away by the noise in our minds. It is a mindful person who can take a step back from the noise and become a distant observer of it instead. If at any point the noise becomes too loud and you feel yourself getting carried away, engage with the feeling of your breath and regain mindfulness of your internal space. This space is your sanctuary. Even if your mind can't be free from noise, you always have the ability to step back and let the noise happen without becoming entangled in it.

3

Body Scan to Release Pain

Sit comfortably. Bring your attention to the top of your head and slowly move it down to your throat, your heart, your belly, your lower abdomen, your hips, your thighs, and all the way down to your feet. Notice what kind of energy is present in each part of your body, as if you were shining a spotlight on what is happening inside you.

Notice if you feel any stagnant energy or pain. And then imagine you are channeling the breath into that specific area, bringing relaxation and ease to anything that may need to be released.

Through this visualization process you are opening yourself up and becoming aware of what is happening inside you. This practice can help you meet aches, pains, stories, imperfections—whatever may be residing in the body and being put out into the world—with an open heart.

4
OCTOBER

Drop the Past

Can you drop all of your past all at once,
and continue to ask for forgiveness?

5
OCTOBER

Sharing Yourself Is Helping Others

Share your truth with others with an open heart.
We are all in this together.

6
OCTOBER

Take Action

Have you noticed that it only takes one little setback for you to launch into victim stories? Victim stories sound like blame, excuses, denial, and defensiveness. Notice when your thoughts go that way, and challenge yourself to try something new. Take responsibility and take action. If you keep the same beliefs and the same behaviors, you'll always have the same results. What can you do differently today to change your situation?

7
OCTOBER

Good Morning

May all parts of yourself awaken to what is already awake within you. You are worthy of enlightenment.

8

Visualization: Stripping Away

With the support of your breath, land back into your body, grounded and supported. Now visualize stripping away everything in your life that is limiting you and preventing you from knowing a deeper and more profound part of yourself. Take notice of how this releasing makes you feel. Cultivate this feeling of releasing everything and being here now. Remember this feeling and carry it with you throughout your day.

9

OCTOBER

Acceptance Affirmation

"I love the parts of myself
that I'm not proud of."

10
OCTOBER

Notice Your Judgment

Notice if you're too quick to judge. You might be operating from your unconscious bias. Today, practice noticing how your judgment or bias impacts your perception of certain people, which aspects of a person you pay attention to, how actively you listen to certain people, and how much or how little you offer kindness to certain people in specific situations.

11
OCTOBER

Start Now

Practicing radical forgiveness gives you freedom from social constructs—an opportunity to start again, knowing that your life is a vast, empty page and that you can write any story you want on it.

12
OCTOBER

Healing Mantra Meditation

Breathing in, say: *I am healing.*

Breathing out, say: *I allow life to work its magic.*

Breathing in: *I release all pain, illness, and heartache from my being.*

Breathing out: *I am safe and in perfect health.*

13
OCTOBER

Everything Counts

Each conscious choice you make is a profound act of generosity not only for yourself, but also for your community and the world at large.

14
OCTOBER

Unhook Yourself

You have the power to stop overreacting to threats and stop feeding the loop of negativity, repeating the same mistakes again and again. Next time you observe that you're becoming hooked on a trigger, engage with your breath and find the opening within you that is untainted by negative bias. It's there.

15
OCTOBER

Yours or Mine?

There will always be a hook to hang your projections on. Today, notice when you're attributing your own repressed feelings to someone else.

16
OCTOBER

Glimpses

You were born with an inherently blissful, compassionate, creative nature. Where did it go?

17
OCTOBER

Choose Wisely

You are the director of your life. You can influence everything around you with the words you speak and the thoughts you hold in your mind. Be responsible and intentional with this power. Speak kindly to yourself and others, and engage with words and thoughts that are filled with loving kindness.

18
OCTOBER

Mastering Confidence

The less you judge yourself, the more confident you become.

19
OCTOBER

Inspiration Affirmation

"I am an inspiration
to someone."

20
OCTOBER

Passing Waves Affirmation

"Today, I am able to discern between
the truth and what is simply present,
no matter how difficult what presents itself
may be. Today, I will not let anxiety
take over, and I will remember
that this too shall pass."

21
OCTOBER

Notice Where You Place Your Energy

You can't be devoted to your healing and to your lies at the same
time. You have to pick one or the other.

22
OCTOBER

Reminders

You carry a divine message for someone.

23
OCTOBER

Operating from the Heart

Despite how compassionate, open, and peaceful you try to be, others can only meet you as deeply as they've met themselves. By attempting to always approach everyone this way, you create the conditions for others to go deeper and in doing so, potentially meet you where you are.

24
OCTOBER

Choose Compassion

When you forgive yourself, you are playing an active role in creating a more compassionate and unified world. It does not mean your past behavior is ignored; it means that you're choosing compassion, freedom, and a more peaceful future.

25
OCTOBER

The Breakthrough

Do you want to know if you've made progress? See if you can forgive people.

26
OCTOBER

One of the Hardest Steps

Give yourself good news: Forgive yourself.

27
OCTOBER

Turn the Spotlight

When anxiety strikes or you become overwhelmed by negative feelings, take a breath and appreciate life outside of yourself by carefully describing what you're seeing.

28
OCTOBER

Kindness Defines You

The moment you realize you are not the mistakes you've made is the moment you can adopt a new and kinder way of being. Let your foundation now be rooted in how kind you can be toward yourself and others.

29
OCTOBER

Be a Hero

Stand in a power pose, with your feet apart, your hands on your hips, and your chin tilted upward. And repeat the mantra, "Today I choose to be a role model."

30

OCTOBER

The Barometer

Are your feelings and thoughts reliable guides?

31

OCTOBER

Loving-Kindness Meditation: Humility

Start by resting your attention on the feeling of the breath in the body. Then gently repeat these phrases:

May I be humble.

May you be humble.

May we be humble.

Now notice how you feel. Repeat this meditation throughout your day, especially when you feel judgment arising within you.

NOVEMBER

—

WHOLENESS

1

The Language of the Heart

Words are limited by our minds, which are dense with old memories, future fantasies, the need to control, and interpretations of the truth rather than truth itself. The heart is more reliable. The language of the heart speaks in beauty and love, but it is much quieter than the language of the mind. We have to get quiet enough to hear it.

2

Caught in a Lie

Because we tend to believe our projections, make a vow to not project your worries onto life or others today.

3

Affirmation for Difficult Times

"I deeply and profoundly send healing and love to all parts of myself that are still experiencing suffering. Even though it is a lot for me to take on, I am doing it anyway."

4
NOVEMBER

Body Scan: Eyes

Start by taking a comfortable seat. Feel your spine—its length and space. Invite relaxation as you bring your attention to your breath, simply following a few cycles of inhaling and exhaling.

Shift your focus to the activity happening around your eyes. Notice the space between each eye, the way the eyelids are resting. Simply observe what is present in that area—the pulsing sensations, perhaps the air touching the skin of your eyelids.

Take this opportunity to rejoice in how precious your body is.

5
NOVEMBER

Growth Opportunity

Empowering others helps you grow.

6
NOVEMBER

Cultural Healing

Your personal healing is helping lessen the weight of any internalized oppression you may be entangled in or you may have unconsciously inherited, even if you are not aware of it. Every time you choose to say a kinder word to yourself or another, you are connecting with this truth.

7
NOVEMBER

Speaking Up for Yourself

Once your mind is trained to disengage from habitual self-critical thinking patterns and behaviors, it's time to figure out how to teach others that you won't be abused. You are strong and assertive enough to stand up for yourself. You are worth it, and what you say matters. The more you practice speaking up for yourself, the easier it becomes.

8

Allowing Grief

Grief visits everyone. No one escapes the pain of grief. It isn't comfortable to sit with grief. We would rather push it away with distractions, or cover the pain with things that bring temporary pleasure.

What if you choose to invite grief in instead? Can you greet grief and offer it tea? See what changes when you invite pain in. It never goes away, but it becomes much less scary, and you become more resilient.

9

Impromptu

Do something good today. Find a way to serve a stranger spontaneously. This will soften your heart and help you cultivate a habit that leads to collective healing.

10
NOVEMBER

Pay Attention to Your Reactions

When a trigger threatens to disturb your peace, practice tracing the activity of your mind and body as the trigger arises. Observe your interpretation of the trigger, then the body's reaction to that thought, and then your urge to act. Acknowledge that you're caught in the cycle of reactivity. With the support of the breath, you can self-regulate and break the cycle by choosing a better response.

11
NOVEMBER

We Are Relational Beings

We are totally interconnected. When you allow your humanity to come into view, you notice that we are co-creating each other at every moment.

Force of Good Affirmation

"I'm here as a force of good. I'm committed to helping the evolution of our society. Nothing and no one can take me away from what I came here to do. I wish peace to all."

13

NOVEMBER

Practice Community

The most radical move we can make is to empower each other, to take care of each other, to practice community, to honor where each one of us is on our unique healing path, and to respect each other's suffering and fragility. This is love. Remember that everyone is on their own path.

14

NOVEMBER

Redesign Your Senses

When you bring the mind to a balance, you start to see, hear, and feel clearly. You are reclaiming agency over your life.

15
NOVEMBER

Your Last Breath

Take a comfortable position, lying down and closing your eyes. Bring your awareness to the sensation of the breath, focusing on this ordinary process of breathing that keeps you alive.

Now visualize yourself on your deathbed. Get into the feeling that these are your last moments on earth; feel death coming closer. Feel the loss of everything you wanted but didn't get, everything you tried to achieve but did not. Feel the death of your aspirations and dreams. Feel the unfinished conversations. What did you want to say to your family and friends or someone you have been fighting with?

Stay connected to the feeling of death coming closer. What are you still holding back? What are you not expressing honestly about yourself? Allow these answers to come to you. This is your last opportunity to come clean with yourself. Get deep into the feeling. What have you been lying about to yourself? How have you self-sabotaged your success? Allow the answers to come to you.

Feel your last breaths of your precious life. Take another breath. What would you like to say to your loved ones? What would you like to say to yourself?

May this practice make clear what is most important to you. To come out of this meditation, take a deep breath, open your eyes, and rejoice in being alive.

16
NOVEMBER

Thinking is Addictive

Obsessive thinking keeps you in a state of unconscious addiction, intoxicated by your fears. Notice when you believe you have no options to choose from; that's when you know you're hooked.

17
NOVEMBER

Micromanaging

Do you constantly wish things to be different than they are?
This need to control causes you to suffer.

18
NOVEMBER

Turn Your Life into
Your Practice Affirmation

"Today I choose to bring
the practice of meditation
into as many areas
of my life as I can."

19
NOVEMBER

Building a New Foundation

Each time you dip into the inner silence of your heart, you are uprooting parts of the old mental architecture. Set aside a few minutes to be in your heart and rebuild the foundation of your castle.

20
NOVEMBER

Learning from Anger

Internal anger always comes out. With meditation, you can re-parent yourself in order to learn from your anger. Give yourself a time-out and make a different choice.

21
NOVEMBER

———

Let Them Be

When you put people in a box, you rob them of their potential for goodness, and you rob yourself of the experience of their goodness.

22
NOVEMBER

———

Consciously Choose Your Motivation

Feelings, good or bad, feel right, so they always motivate you one way or another. With practice, you can change your relationship with your feelings and reclaim your power to choose which ones are good guides for you to follow.

23
NOVEMBER

The Human Condition

Cultivate a life where you don't always expect everyone to feel great all the time. You and everyone else have to feel feelings in order to process them and allow them to pass. Feelings only get stronger if you push them aside or avoid them.

24
NOVEMBER

Smile Visualization

Offer your mind a treat: Visualize yourself with a huge smile, free of all anxiety and fear.

25
NOVEMBER

Watch Your Mind's Stories

Practice noticing the stories that play out in your mind when feelings arise. Observe that even good feelings can be followed by damaging thoughts.

26
NOVEMBER

Merging the Inner and Outer Worlds

Being mindful internally and externally at the same time is a practice of remembering to rely on yourself while fully participating in the world.

27
NOVEMBER

—

Rebirth Meditation

Start by resting your attention on the feeling of the breath in the body. Then gently repeat these phrases:

May I be reborn in a totally new way.

May you be reborn in a totally new way.

May we be reborn in a totally new way.

Now notice how you feel. Repeat this meditation throughout your day, especially in difficult or challenging interpersonal situations.

28
NOVEMBER

Inner Pause Button

Notice how most decisions you need to make are not urgent ones. Take a breath and recompose yourself before acting. Taking those extra few seconds allows you to break free from the involuntary think-feel-react habit.

29
NOVEMBER

Now Is the Time

Your opportunity to let go and trust is now.

30
NOVEMBER

Who Supports You?

We are inherently social beings, and our experience in relationships can define who we are. Because we are designed to connect, notice the people in your life who support your healing and those who frown upon your desire to change. Take this opportunity to do a relationship inventory.

DECEMBER

RETURNING TO THE HEART

1
DECEMBER

Gifts of Grace

If you've found yourself constantly looking around for threats and wrongs, take a vow that today you'll look around for gifts of grace.

2
DECEMBER

You Are Never Alone

Life is always talking to you. Practice observing the signs and messages; they are reminders that you are totally interconnected and you are never alone. You just have to remember how to tune in and listen. Throughout the day, with the support of your breath, drop from the mind into the heart and see the universe responding to you.

3

DECEMBER

Alignment Affirmation

"Today I choose to let go of my past and align myself with the highest harmonies. May this open me up to my essence and invoke my power."

4

Loving-Kindness Meditation: Trauma

Start by resting your attention on the feeling of the breath in the body. Then gently repeat these phrases:

May I let go of my traumas.

May you let go of your traumas.

May we let go of our traumas.

Now notice how you feel. Repeat this meditation throughout your day, but especially if you notice yourself feeling triggered by a past event.

5
DECEMBER

Give Away Your Gifts

In helping others, you find truth.

In seeing others, you find yourself.

In helping others, you find the missing pieces to your healing.

In acknowledging others, you come into close contact with grace.

And if you want to keep these gifts, you must continue to give yours away.

6
DECEMBER

How Does It Make You Feel?

Certain things feel good, but they might not be good for you. Notice how you feel after the fact: Do you feel depleted or empowered?

7
DECEMBER

Body Scan Meditation: Rib Cage

Close your eyes and bring your attention to your rib cage, first the left side and then the right side. Feel the breath filling the spaces between each rib on the left and right sides. With each breath in, notice the lungs expanding outward toward the rib cage, and with each breath out, notice the lungs contracting inward away from the rib cage. Stay with this feeling for the remainder of your five-minute practice.

8
DECEMBER

Expand to All Beings

Expand your sense of self so much that you can include nature, the oceans, your close ones and kindred spirits across the world, all beings everywhere, known and unknown.

9
DECEMBER

Who Am I?

Practice asking yourself, "Who am I?" Allow the answers to come to you. Do this diligently, and an inner peace will arise from the mind experiencing its essence.

10
DECEMBER

Engaging from Peace

What would it feel like to engage with the world all the time from a place of peace? What is stopping you?

11
DECEMBER

Trust Affirmation

Today I wish for more trust.

I trust that when doors close, new ones open twofold.

I trust that when people leave my life, it's for my growth and transformation.

I trust that everything I need or will ever need is within me now.

I trust that my ideas matter.

I trust that helping others rise is how I rise.

I trust the path I'm walking.

12
DECEMBER

The Need for Approval

Have you considered that past humiliation could show up in the present as a desperate need for validation? Shame has many faces, and this is one. Notice when you're doing things out of the need for approval. Take a breath and say, "I approve of myself."

13
DECEMBER

Forgiveness Is a Quality of the Brave

If you're seeking forgiveness, you have to search for ways you can create that for other people. Help others forgive. If you want to help yourself, forgive.

14
DECEMBER

The Library

There comes a time when you are able to look at your own traumas as if you were reading a book about someone else's life. It becomes a choice to walk over to the bookshelf and pick up that dusty old book or start a new book.

15
DECEMBER

Doubting Peace

We are accustomed to overcomplicating and overanalyzing, so when we find peace in simplicity, we start to entertain the idea that this simplicity can't actually be peace. But it can.

16

DECEMBER

Creative Exchange Visualization

Take a comfortable seat. Now close your eyes and take three long deep breaths to release the body and mind of any tension.

Now begin to visualize someone that embodies compassion, wisdom, and power sitting right here in front of you.

Breathe in and out from your heart center.

Breathe in and visualize receiving compassion, wisdom, and power in the form of golden purifying light from their heart into yours.

As you exhale, visualize dark smoke moving out of your body, releasing with it all the things that do not serve you.

Continue this creative exchange for a few minutes. With every inhale and exhale you are purifying and cleansing your mind and awakening your innate compassion, wisdom, power, and light.

17
DECEMBER

The Root

We are conditioned to believe that our happiness is dependent on people, places, and things. This belief makes us keep a tight grip on the world, demanding it be as we expect it to be, allowing no room for change. Such clinging leads to unnecessary suffering. In which areas of your life could you loosen this attachment?

18
DECEMBER

The Beauty Outside Yourself

When you're snagged in thoughts about the future and you feel anxiety creeping up, take a breath and practice immersing yourself in the beauty outside of you. This will realign you with your heart, and solutions beyond logic will arise.

19
DECEMBER

Imposter Syndrome

Do you feel unworthy of the praise you receive for your accomplishments and refuse to accept it? To the world, you're probably doing a good job at accepting the praise, but internally you are questioning your worth and legitimacy.

Here's your reminder that you're not a fraud. With the support of your breath, become mindful of your impact by taking a view from the outside looking in. You will see that you're not the unlovable failure you believe yourself to be. To reinforce this practice, write down a list of five accomplishments you're proud of.

20
DECEMBER

Recovery Affirmation

"It takes courage to put myself back together. I'm slowly recovering from my addiction to suffering."

21
DECEMBER

A Quick Return to Self

How do you come back to the love inside of you? Forgive yourself a little bit every day. Engage the breath and repeat in your mind: *Any harm I have caused others, may they forgive me. Any harm I have caused myself, I forgive myself.*

22
DECEMBER

―

Wholeness Affirmation

"I, [*your name*], see, hear, feel,
and know that I am whole!"

23
DECEMBER

―

Beyond Thoughts

When you enter the present moment, notice how your mind is free of aversions. In that freedom you have access to a realm where beauty, creativity, joy, and inner peace arise.

24
DECEMBER

———

You Are Enough

For today, commit to stop searching for outside validation. Support your intention with this breathing meditation.

Breathing in, say: *I am*

Breathing out, say: *Enough.*

Breathing in: *Where I am*

Breathing out: *Is enough.*

25
DECEMBER

———

Measure the Depth of Your Love

Get out of your own way and drop into your heart. When you arrive, measure the depth of your love. This will dictate how fully you are living.

26
DECEMBER

Healing Energy Affirmation

"With each step today, I send
healing energy directly to the
part of me that needs it most."

27
DECEMBER

Dear Nemesis

Befriend the vicious voice in your mind. Address it with compassion and
forgiveness. Only then can you have healthy relationships with other people.

28
DECEMBER

Be Fully Here

You can't be in the past, present, and future at the same time.
Be fully here. Otherwise life passes you by.

29
DECEMBER

The Perpetual Assessment

As you come in contact with people, places, and things, practice simply
paying attention without getting carried away in judging everyone
and everything.

30
DECEMBER

Fifty Promises

Dear [*your name*], this year I promise:

1. to nurture myself when I feel depleted.

2. to be open to surprise.

3. to learn from my mistakes.

4. to forgive and seek forgiveness.

5. to believe in myself.

6. to look within when I feel triggered.

7. to tell the truth.

8. to stop comparing myself to everyone.

9. to explore new ideas often.

Continued

10. to let go of expectations.

11. to not worry about what other people might think or say about me.

12. to stop all hateful thoughts.

13. to believe in my own path.

14. to avoid trying to make things perfect.

15. to not live anywhere but in the Now.

16. to work outside my comfort zone.

17. to love simplicity.

18. to laugh often.

19. to surround myself with good people.

20. to speak up.

21. to live in balance.

22. to take care of my body.

23. to accept the mystery.

24. to stop thinking this is a dress rehearsal.

25. to not believe everything I think.

26. to not believe that every feeling is the right guide to my life.

27. to say no to people who constantly dump on my healing.

28. to cry often.

29. to be in nature often.

30. to accept myself completely.

31. to check in with the inner me often.

32. to keep going.

33. to know that my past does not define who I am.

34. to ask for help and help others when I can.

35. to embrace my imperfections.

36. to start again, stronger each time.

37. to express gratitude often.

Continued

38. to be flexible.

39. to be patient.

40. to practice random acts of kindness.

41. to develop healing strategies for coping with pain and suffering.

42. to cultivate moments of flow.

43. to stop talking down to myself.

44. to stop trying to be someone I'm not.

45. to remember that everything is temporary.

46. to accept change.

47. to help others feel good.

48. to love deeper each day.

49. to believe wholeheartedly in my goodness.

50. to delight in my own magic often.

31
DECEMBER

New Year Visualization

Where were you last New Year's Eve? Allow the moments of bliss from your past year to flash by like a highlight reel in your mind. Then allow a highlight reel of the moments of sadness to flash in your mind. Now express gratitude for all of it, and ask yourself, "What is the biggest lesson I learned from this year?"

Take a long deep breath in, and as you breathe out, visualize letting go of anything that could be an impediment to you having your best year yet. Breathing in, ask yourself, "What do I want to cultivate in the coming year?" Allow the answers to come to you.

Take a moment to engage with the joy that comes with this vision filled with blessings and lessons. Take a breath, and as you inhale, send a blessing to every situation coming to you in the new year.

FURTHER READING

Chödrön, Pema. *How to Meditate: A Practical Guide to Making Friends with Your Mind.* Boulder, CO: Sounds True, 2013.

Dass, Ram. *Journey of Awakening: A Meditator's Guidebook.* New York, NY: Bantam, 1990.

Gyatso, Geshe Kelsang. *The New Heart of Wisdom: Profound Teachings from Buddha's Heart.* Glen Spey, NY: Tharpa Publications, 2012.

Hanh, Thich Nhat. *The Miracle of Mindfulness: An Introduction to the Practice of Meditation.* Boston, MA: Beacon Press, 1991.

Hanh, Thich Nhat. *Peace Is Every Step: The Path of Mindfulness in Everyday Life.* New York, NY: Bantam, 1991.

Kabat-Zinn, Jon. *Wherever You Go, There You Are: Mindfulness Meditation in Everyday Life.* New York, NY: Hachette, 2005.

Kornfield, Jack. *A Path with Heart: A Guide Through the Perils and Promises of Spiritual Life.* New York, NY: Bantam, 1993.

Salzberg, Sharon. *Real Happiness: The Power of Meditation.* New York, NY: Workman, 2010.

Suzuki, Shunryu. *Zen Mind, Beginner's Mind: Informal Talks on Zen Meditation and Practice.* Boulder, CO: Shambhala, 2011.

Wallace, B. Alan *The Attention Revolution: Unlocking the Power of the Focused Mind.* Somerville, WI: Wisdom Publications, 2006.

Warner, Brad. *Sit Down and Shut Up: Punk Rock Commentaries on Buddha, God, Truth, Sex, Death, and Dogen's Treasury of the Right Dharma Eye.* Berkeley, CA: New World Library, 2007.

ACKNOWLEDGMENTS

I would like to express deep gratitude for Meg Ilasco for asking me to write this book, and to my editor, Melissa Valentine, for her support and for being an all-around superstar. I want to thank my sister, Moun D'Simone, for being my biggest cheerleader and for always pushing me to tell my deepest truth. To mom, dad, and my little brother, Micky—you're my rocks; without you, there is no story. To all my teachers, I would not be here if it weren't for you: His Holiness the Dalai Lama, Lama Zopa Rinpoche, Krishna Das, Venerable Joan Nicell, Ram Dass, Thubten Gyatso, Geshe Gelon Sonam, Amma, Govin Sharan, Sharon Salzberg, Gesge Kelsang Wangmo, Richard P. Brown, MD; Joe Loizzo, MD, PhD; Dr. Miles Neale. Thank you from the bottom of my heart to Luke Simon, Lisa Levine, Katia Tallarico, and Brett Bevell for giving me my first opportunity to teach. And my dearest friends Gabriel Marques, Ruby Warrington, Lakshmi Junia, Ashish Gupta, and Tiffany Kappeler, I love you! To all the incredible people along my travels, thank you all for being a pivotal part of my journey.

ABOUT THE AUTHOR

SAH D'SIMONE is a meditation teacher, author, transformational speaker, and coach who has dedicated his life to helping others to live in alignment and achieve their highest potential. His infectious enthusiasm for healing and self-love is grounded in a masterful synthesis of the ancient modalities of meditation, contemplative psychotherapy, breath work, and plant-based nutrition for a modern and accessible approach to well-being. Sah teaches around the world, sharing his mission of healing, mental health, and well-being with all, including Fortune 500 companies, LGBTIQ, underserved, and POC communities alike. Find out more at SahDSimone.com or stay connected on his Instagram, @SahDSimone.